FOOTBALL LEGENDS

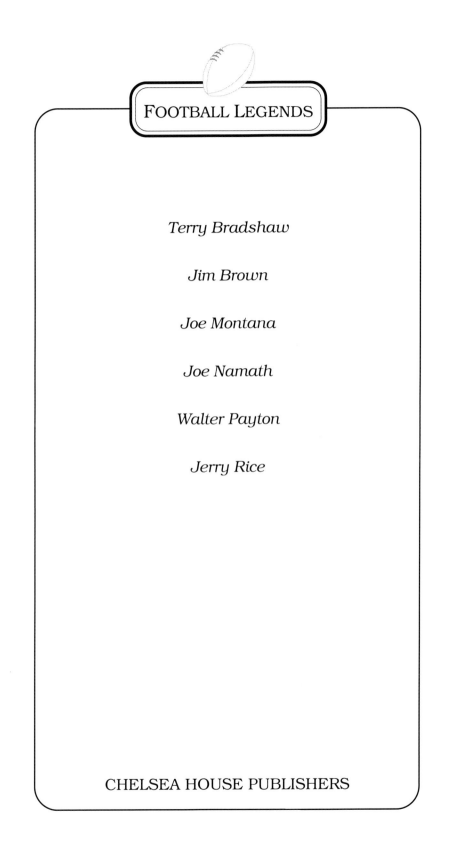

Terry Bradshaw

Jim Brown

Joe Montana

Joe Namath

Walter Payton

Jerry Rice

CHELSEA HOUSE PUBLISHERS

FOOTBALL LEGENDS

JIM BROWN

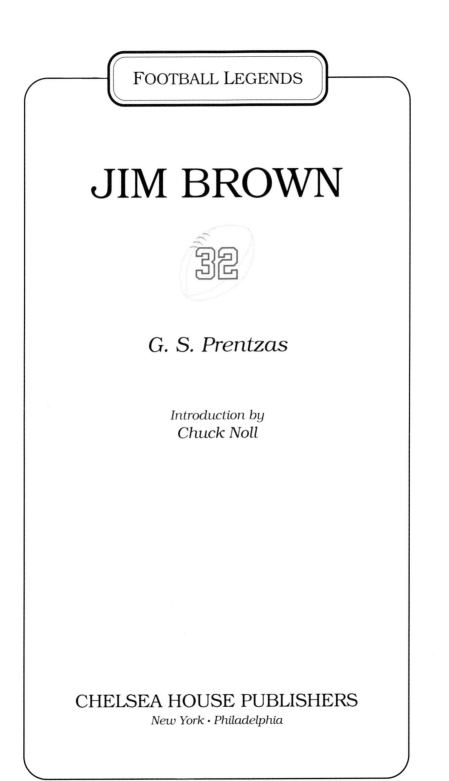

G. S. Prentzas

Introduction by
Chuck Noll

CHELSEA HOUSE PUBLISHERS
New York • Philadelphia

Produced by Daniel Bial and Associates
New York, New York.

Picture research by Alan Gottlieb
Cover illustration by Fred Willingham

1 3 5 7 9 8 6 4 2

Prentzas, G. S.
    Jim Brown / Scott Prentzas.
        p.   cm. — (Football legends)
    Includes bibliographical references (p.) and index.
    ISBN 0-7910-2452-0
    1. Brown, Jim, 1936–   —Juvenile literature. 2. Football
players—United States—Biography—Juvenile literature. 3. National
Football League—Juvenile literature. [1. Brown, Jim, 1936–
2. Football players. 3. Afro-Americans—Biography.] I. Title.
II. Series.
GV939.B75P74   1994
796.332′092—dc20
    [B]   94-1349
                                                                  CIP
                                                                   AC

CONTENTS

A WINNING ATTITUDE

Chuck Noll

Don't ever fall into the trap of believing, "I could never do that. And I won't even try—I don't want to embarrass myself." After all, most top athletes had no idea what they could accomplish when they were young. A secret to the success of every star quarterback and sure-handed receiver is that they tried. If they had not tried, if they had not persevered, they would never have discovered how far they could go and how much they could achieve.

You can learn about trying hard and overcoming challenges by being a sports fan. Or you can take part in organized sports at any level, in any capacity. The student messenger at my high school is now president of a university. A reserve ballplayer who got very little playing time in high school now owns a very successful business. Both of them benefited by the lesson of perseverance that sports offers. The main point is that you don't have to be a Hall of Fame athlete to reap the benefits of participating in sports.

In math class, I learned that the whole is equal to the sum of its parts. But that is not always the case when you are dealing with people. Sports has taught me that the whole is either greater than or less than the sum of its parts, depending on how well the parts work together. And how the parts work together depends on how they really understand the concept of teamwork.

Most people believe that teamwork is a fifty-fifty proposition. But true teamwork is seldom, if ever, fifty-fifty. Teamwork is *whatever it takes to get the job done.* There is no time for the measurement of contributions, no time for anything but concentrating on your job.

One year, my Pittsburgh Steelers were playing the Houston Oilers in the Astrodome late in the season, with the division championship on the line. Our offensive line was hard hit by the flu, our starting quarterback was out with an injury, and we were having difficulty making a first down. There was tremendous pressure on our defense to perform well—and they rose to the occasion. If the players on the defensive unit had been measuring their contribution against the offense's contribution, they would have given up and gone home. Instead, with a "whatever it takes" attitude, they increased their level of concentration and performance, forced turnovers, and got the ball into field goal range for our offense. Thanks to our defense's winning attitude, we came away with a victory.

Believing in doing whatever it takes to get the job done is what separates a successful person from someone who is not as successful. Nobody can give you this winning outlook; you have to develop it. And I know from experience that it can be learned and developed on the playing field.

My favorite people on the football field have always been offensive linemen and defensive backs. I say this because it takes special people to perform well in jobs in which there is little public recognition when they are doing things right but are thrust into the spotlight as soon as they make a mistake. That is exactly what happens to a lineman whose man sacks the quarterback or a defensive back who lets his receiver catch a touchdown pass. They know the importance of being part of a group that believes in teamwork and does not point fingers at one another.

Sports can be a learning situation as much as it can be fun. And that's why I say, "Get involved. Participate."

CHUCK NOLL, the Pittsburgh Steelers head coach from 1969–1991, led his team to four Super Bowl victories—the most by any coach. Widely respected as an innovator on both offense and defense, Noll was inducted into the Pro Football Hall of Fame in 1993.

1

THE CHAMPIONSHIP

On Sunday, December 27, 1964, nearly 80,000 football fans jammed into Cleveland Municipal Stadium to watch the hometown Browns take on the Baltimore Colts for the championship of the National Football League (NFL). The 20-mile-per-hour wind blowing off Lake Erie rippled the flags above the stadium and chilled the anxious crowd. The temperature hovered around the freezing mark when the Browns, in their home white uniforms, and the Colts, wearing their dark blue road jerseys, took the field.

At that time, the NFL championship game was pro football's big event. The rival American Football League (AFL) had begun play in 1960, but the first Super Bowl would not be held for another two years, and it would take till the end of the decade before the AFL proved it could match up against the best NFL teams.

Many legends of the game—including Red Grange, Bronko Nagurski, Sammy Baugh,

Jim Brown gaining a first down in the 1964 title game, which he called "the high point of my career."

The Browns' Lou "the Toe" Groza scored the first points against a Colts team that had not been shut out in 31 games and had never before lost a championship game.

Bobby Layne, and Chuck Bednarik—had displayed their talents in the NFL championship game, and this year was no different. The Browns were led by superstar fullback Jim Brown, speedy rookie receiver Paul Warfield, and Lou "The Toe" Groza, a paunchy 40-year-old place kicker. The Colts' roster featured future Hall of Famers Johnny Unitas at quarterback, Lenny Moore at halfback, Raymond Berry at end, and Gino Marchetti at defensive end.

Perhaps no other player on the field hungered for a victory more than Brown. Although he held most of the NFL career records for carrying the ball, Brown had never won an NFL championship. Some critics suggested that the most feared runner in the game was not a team player. In newspapers, bars, and schoolyards in Cleveland and across the country, people accused Brown of putting individual achievements above team goals.

Since Brown had arrived in Cleveland in 1957, the Browns were always one of the best teams in the league, but they had played in the title game only once, his rookie season. The team lost that game, and the prospects for victory did not look good this time around. Cleveland had a potent offense, capturing the Eastern Conference crown with a 10-3-1 record. But the defensive unit—a collection of aging linemen, undersized linebackers, and short defensive backs—had yielded a lot of points during the regular season. So in a late-season trade with the New York Giants, the Browns acquired Dick Modzelewski, a stumpy, no-neck defensive tackle who had earned a reputation as a tough defender against the run. The Browns hoped that the 12-year veteran would provide the defense with the leadership that the unit desperately needed.

In contrast, the Colts' offensive and defensive units both dominated the opposition. The team had easily won the Western Conference, posting an impressive 12-2 record. Unitas, the premier quarterback of the era, directed an offensive machine that featured a precision passing attack and a powerful running game. The team scored 428 points in 14 regular season games, an average of 30.5 points a game. The Colts' defense gave up fewer points than any team in the league in 1964 and always put intense pressure on the opposing quarterback.

As a result, the Colts were prohibitive favorites. Except for the Browns players and their diehard fans, almost everyone expected a rout. After assessing the strengths and weaknesses of the two teams, a *Sports Illustrated* writer confidently predicted that "although the Browns are a sound, intelligent and even explosive football team, they stand small chance of upsetting the Colts." But all the predictions, analysis, and hoopla meant nothing once the game began.

For some fans, the first half proved to be a gripping defensive struggle; for others, it was a dull spectacle. The blustery wind played havoc with the quarterbacks' passes, and both offenses chose to play conservatively. The Colts mounted the lone scoring threat in the half, driving the ball to the Browns' 22 yardline early in the second quarter. Their left-footed kicker, Lou Michaels, lined up for a field goal attempt, but the holder fumbled the snap and was quickly buried under a sea of white uniforms. The half ended in a scoreless tie. The two defenses had played well: The Colts had limited the dangerous Jim Brown to 43 yards on 11 carries, and the Browns had bridled the high-power Colt offense.

The Colts received the second-half kickoff but could not move the ball against the charged-up Browns defense. Their punter managed only a 25-yard kick into the strong headwind, and Cleveland began its first series of the second half on the Baltimore 48 yardline. When the Colts stymied the Browns' drive, Lou Groza, the oldest player in the league, booted a 43-yard field goal with the wind at his back, giving the home team a 3-0 lead.

Following another failed Colts series, Cleveland took over on its own 33 yardline. The second play of the drive proved to be the turning point in the game. With the ball situated on the left hash mark, the Browns set up in a double-wing formation, which left Jim Brown as the only man in the backfield behind quarterback Frank Ryan. The Colts adjusted their defense to the wide side of the field, where the Browns had the most room to run or attempt a pass. When the ball was snapped, Ryan quickly pitched the

pigskin to Brown, who went barreling to the *left*, away from the Baltimore defenders positioned on the other side of the field. With three blockers in front of him, Brown shot past the linebackers and rambled for 46 yards before a speedy Baltimore defensive back dragged him down from behind.

On the next play, the confused Colts keyed on Brown, expecting another run. Instead, Ryan faded back into the pocket and threw a bullet to flanker Gary Collins, who had run a post pattern and was wide open in the end zone. With those two plays, Cleveland seized the momentum, and they would never relinquish it. Ryan threw two more touchdown passes to Collins, and Brown bulldozed his way through the defense as the Browns rolled to an

Browns quarterback Frank Ryan cursed the wind in the first half, but then figured out a way to lead his team to the 1964 NFL title.

unthinkable 27-0 lead over the heavily favored Colts. In the waning moments of the game, a stampede of delirious Browns fans streamed onto the field and jubilantly ripped down the west goal posts. In the midst of the mayhem, the officials prudently shot off the gun to end the game, even though 26 seconds remained on the clock.

In the victors' lockerroom, the players expressed their joy and relief. In upsetting the Colts, the Browns had overcome their individual and collective demons. For Jim Brown, the victory was particularly sweet. "It was the high point of my career," he recalled in his autobiography, *Out of Bounds*. "We finally won the big one and mission was accomplished."

Brown had made a substantial contribution to the win, gaining 114 yards on 21 rushing attempts and catching 3 passes for 37 yards. But he was more pleased with the team effort. His teammates had stepped up in the big game. Surprising the Colts with blitzes and tight pass coverage, the much-maligned Browns defense limited the Colts to 171 total yards, snagged two interceptions, and recovered a Lenny Moore fumble. On offense, Frank Ryan engineered a brilliant attack, Lou Groza contributed two field goals and three extra points, and Gary Collins won the Most Valuable Player award on the strength of his three touchdown catches.

Jim Brown was relieved finally to have won a championship; his critics could no longer say that he never won the big one. In his autobiography he observed, "Unless he wins a championship, even a superstar is never fully accepted. Some people use the absence of a title to criticize a successful individual. They say a team *can't* win a championship with him. He's too much of a soloist."

The 1964 championship proved to be the only championship in Jim Brown's career; he retired after playing one more season. Although he quit the game while he was still in his prime, Brown left behind a stunning record of achievement and established the standard by which NFL running backs are judged. Over the course of nine seasons, Brown set the existing record for every career category in running a football, including most yards gained, average yards per carry, and most rushing touchdowns. Brown led the NFL in rushing and was named to the All-NFL team in eight of his nine years in the league. He was inducted into the Pro Football Hall of Fame in 1971.

Toughness and durability were the qualities that set Brown apart as a football player. Standing 6' 2" and wielding 228 pounds of solid muscle, he had a body that could withstand the punishment that running backs take in the NFL. In many instances, he delivered as much pain as he received. Brown never missed a game, a remarkable feat in an era in which rough play was routine and cheap shots were largely overlooked. Brown played in 118 straight regular season games and 4 post-season games. He left the field only once in his career, when he was kicked in the head in the first half of a 1959 game. He returned to play in the second half. In the minds of many fans, football players do not come any better.

But Jim Brown is much more than just a football legend. He quit the game in 1966 to pursue an acting career. He became Hollywood's first black male sex symbol, appearing in more than

20 films. His starring roles in such action films as *Slaughter* and *Black Gunn* paved the way for many other black actors to find work in the film industry. Muscular and mean-faced, Brown often portrayed strong, violent men in movies.

Brown also became well-known for his incisive views on American society and for his social activism. The football legend and movie star used his celebrity status to bring attention to a wide range of social issues. A complex, thoughtful, and outspoken man, he has been an articulate and often controversial commentator on such topics as racism, sex, drugs, sports, and the media.

A long-time supporter of the black community, Brown has been involved in several organizations that have provided assistance to African Americans. Brown formed the Black Economic Union (BEU), an organization that emphasized economic development for African Americans. The BEU, which opened offices across the nation in the mid-1960s, helped young black businesspeople get their companies started. He also served as executive director of Vital Issues, a program that taught prison inmates self-control and self-reliance.

In the early 1990s, Brown started Amer-I-Can, a self-help program aimed at prison inmates and street gang members. Taking a personal interest in helping inner city kids, he continues to walk the streets of Los Angeles' ghettos, talking to young people and inviting them to his home to take part in Amer-I-Can sessions.

As an athlete, actor, businessman, and social activist, Jim Brown has always shown a fierce dedication to getting the job done. Whether it has

WHAT DOES THE FUTUR HOLD FOR ME ?

meant taking on a linebacker, speaking out against racism, or making a human connection with a gang member, he has confidently accepted the challenge and overcome whatever obstacles have blocked his path to success.

Jim Brown on his way to the offices of the Black Economic Union shortly after retiring from football.

2
GROWING UP

James Nathaniel Brown was born on February 17, 1936, on St. Simons Island, Georgia. According to the stories that Jim heard, his father, Swinton Brown, had been an amateur football player and a prizefighter. He was also a free spirit and never settled down with Jim and his mother, Theresa. Swinton moved north when Jim was young. He eventually married another woman and started a family with her. Jim saw his father only three or four times, and he never felt close to him.

When Jim was two years old, Theresa Brown left her young son in the care of her grandmother, Nora Peterson. Because jobs were scarce on St. Simons Island, Theresa moved to New York to work as a maid for a family on Long Island. Jim missed his mother, but his great-grandmother promised the youngster that he would be reunited with her someday.

Jim Brown was named best athlete in his high school yearbook (shown here with the best female athlete in his class).

Jim found himself without either of his parents, and his great-grandmother became the most important person in his life. Nora Peterson earned a meager living as a domestic, but she always managed to provide everything that Jim needed—food, clothes, and, most importantly, love. In *Out of Bounds*, Brown fondly recalled his childhood: "I've never felt more love than I did as a child on St. Simons Island. The black folks on the island would watch out for their neighbors." He never forgot the values that his great-grandmother instilled in him and the sense of community that he experienced on St. Simons Island.

Jim enjoyed playing with his friends, shooting slingshots, making paper boats, and frolicking along the beach. But when he was eight years old, he boarded a train and left his Georgia childhood behind. As his great-grandmother had always promised, Jim's mother wanted her son to join her up north.

Theresa Brown worked as a maid for a white family, the Brockmans, in Great Neck, New York. She and Jim lived in an apartment over the Brockmans' garage. For the first time in his life, Jim was exposed to the world of white Americans. Some whites lived on St. Simons island, but Jim had few white friends to play with. The Brockmans helped make Jim's transition into this new world easier. They treated Jim and his mother with respect.

When Jim was about to enter high school, however, the Brockmans moved to California. His mother found a new job, and she and Jim moved into an apartment in Manhasset, a nearby town. Jim enrolled at Manhasset High School, which was well regarded for its acade-

mics and its athletics. Jim was one of the school's few black students, but because of his athletic skills, he was soon accepted by the student body and the community.

Like many teenagers, Jim experienced some trying times during his high school years. He and some other athletes started a gang called the Gaylords. Jim was elected president. Compared to many of today's gangs, the Gaylords were not particularly menacing. They mostly cruised around looking for girls. The Gaylords carried switchblades in their pockets but never used them. About the only trouble that they got into was the occasional fist fight with boys from nearby high schools. Some of the Gaylords later fell into a life of crime, but Jim quit the gang before running afoul of the law.

The most difficult period of Jim's high school years began near the end of his junior year. He and his mother had been quarreling about her new boyfriend for weeks. Jim hated the guy. One

Jim Brown (number 11) once scored 55 points in a high school football game.

night he told his mother that he would beat up her boyfriend if he showed up at the apartment again. Jim's mother replied that if he did not like the situation, he could leave. And that's what Jim did. He moved in with the family of his girlfriend.

At Manhasset High, Jim excelled at sports, earning 13 letters. He played on the football, lacrosse, basketball, baseball, and track teams. In his senior year, Jim earned all-state honors in football, basketball, and track. He averaged nearly 15 yards per carry as a halfback and averaged 38 points a game as a basketball forward—amazing statistics both.

Jim also did well in the classroom. His football coach, Ed Walsh, told his star running back that he had the talent to play professional football. But to get there, Walsh pointed out, Jim would have to go to college. To get into college, he would have to make good grades. Walsh's advice motivated the young athlete. Jim hit the books hard, earning a B- average despite participating in so many sports.

Many college coaches and professional scouts approached Jim. It seemed that everyone wanted the high school star to play for them. The New York Yankees offered Jim a minor league baseball contract, but he turned down the offer because he wanted to play college football. "I preferred the physicality and excitement of football," Brown later recalled.

Forty-five colleges offered Brown a football scholarship. Ed Walsh recommended that Jim accept the offer made by Ohio State University coach Woody Hayes. Walsh pointed out that Ohio State was a good place to get an education and that it played in the Big Ten, the nation's premier collegiate football conference at the time. Walsh wanted his star to measure his talent against the very best competition.

But Jim ended up turning down Ohio State's offer. Kenneth Molloy, a Manhasset High booster and one of Brown's mentors, urged Jim to consider Syracuse University. Molloy had played lacrosse at Manhasset High and Syracuse, and he was a staunch supporter of the athletic programs at both schools. Molloy argued that Syracuse was much closer to home than Ohio State; it had a good lacrosse team that Jim could join; and the university was in the process of building a big-time football program. Molloy was certain that the Manhasset High star would be one of the program's key building blocks. Brown found Molloy's arguments convincing and chose to attend Syracuse.

3

ORANGE AND BLACK

At the end of the summer of 1953, Jim Brown packed his bags and headed off to college. He looked forward to a new world of athletics, academics, and independence. He settled into his dormitory, a row of converted barracks on a hill overlooking the city. The dorm, known as Skytop, was located about three miles from the Syracuse University campus. Brown found it strange that no other athletes lived at Skytop.

On his first day of practice, Brown realized that he was the freshman team's only black player. (Before NCAA rules were changed in 1972, freshmen could not play on varsity athletic teams.) He shrugged that off, but then he learned that all of the other freshman players lived in a dorm in the middle of the campus. The other players also had meal tickets to eat in a different campus cafeteria than Brown. Brown sensed that he was being treated differently because of his race.

Besides basketball, football, and lacrosse, Brown was a member of the Syracuse University track team and finished fifth in the NCAA decathlon championship.

His suspicions were confirmed when two coaches and the team's quarterback warned Brown that he better not behave like Vada Stone. Brown had never heard of Stone, but he soon found out that Stone was a black quarterback who had played for the Orangemen two years earlier. He had irritated many whites with his flamboyant style and absolutely enraged them by dating the head majorette, who was white. Stone eventually left Syracuse before graduating to play in the Canadian Football League. Brown realized that everyone thought that because he was black he would be a "troublemaker" like Vada Stone.

During his years living on Long Island, Brown had never encountered a serious racial problem. As he recalled in *Out of Bounds*:

> When I came to Manhasset High School, I was never denied an opportunity. I was living among all these white people, receiving all this warmth and goodness. It lulled me to sleep. I believed everyone would be as good as the people of Manhasset. I came to Syracuse with my guard down. At eighteen, I wasn't prepared for their venom.

Matters were even more complicated than Brown realized. He later learned that he was not at Syracuse on a football scholarship at all. When Kenneth Molloy tried to get Brown a scholarship, the Syracuse coaching staff told him that they had used up all of the scholarships available for that year. Besides, they said, they would not be interested in a player from Long Island, no matter how good his statistics were. Long Island, a region of mostly affluent suburbs, did not have a reputation for producing tough, rugged football players.

What the Syracuse coaches did not tell Molloy was that, after the Vada Stone experience, they did not want any black players on their team. But Molloy persisted. He convinced a group of Manhasset business leaders to contribute to a scholarship fund for Jim Brown. Molloy then struck a deal with the Syracuse coaches: If the Manhasset backers financed Brown's freshman year and if the Manhasset star impressed the coaches, then Syracuse would give him a full scholarship. The coaches reluctantly agreed, and Molloy gathered the funds for Brown's tuition and living expenses. He did not tell Brown about this arrangement because he wanted Jim to think that he had earned a scholarship on his own merits. Molloy was certain that Brown would be an instant success and earn the scholarship.

But at practice, the coaches basically ignored the black, non-scholarship player. One coach told Brown that he would never make it as a runner and encouraged him to switch to another position, perhaps lineman. Another coach suggested that he would make a good punter. Brown tried to ignore these comments because he desperately wanted to show the coaches that he was a gifted runner. But each day wore him down bit by bit. It became harder and harder to make the three-mile trek to practice only to be overlooked and humiliated. Eventually, Brown began to doubt his own abilities and concluded that he was not good enough to play college ball.

He called Kenneth Molloy and told him that he had decided to quit the team. Molloy immediately telephoned Dr. Raymond Collins, the superintendent of the Manhasset school system. Through his son, one of Jim's high school football teammates, Collins had befriended Brown years earlier. He immediately drove to Syracuse to talk to the perplexed young man. Collins convinced Jim to stay on the team, telling him that he had the talent to make it and would prove it if only he would remain patient and keep trying.

Encouraged by Collins's pep talk, Jim stuck it out and survived his freshman year. Before he returned to home for the summer, Jim was summoned to the office of varsity head coach Ben Schwartzwalder. The coach told Brown that he wanted him on the team next year but that he wanted Jim to switch from running back to receiver. Jim insisted on being a running back, and after much debate Schwartzwalder agreed to give him a shot as a runner.

When Brown returned to Syracuse for varsity practice at the end of the summer, he discovered that Schwartzwalder had indeed listed him as a halfback—on the fifth string. He did not play in the first three games of the season, but in the fourth game against Illinois, Jim got to start because most of the team's running backs were injured. He also played a few downs at cornerback in the game and made several ferocious hits.

Going into the sixth game of the season, Jim was listed as the second-string halfback. The starters were not having much success running against the stubborn Cornell University defense. Restless fans started chanting, "We want Brown! We want Brown!" A shiver ran down Jim's spine. A few minutes later, the starting halfback injured his ankle, and the coaches sent Brown into the game. On his first carry, Brown ripped through the Big Red defense for a 54-yard touchdown run. The crowd went bonkers. Jim racked up 150 yards for the game. Not surpris-

ingly, he started every game for the rest of his
collegiate career. In his three varsity seasons
(1954-56), Brown amassed 2,091 rushing yards
and scored 25 touchdowns.

In his senior year, Brown earned All-American honors. He ran for 986 yards in eight
games, averaging 6.2 yards per carry. In his final
game, Brown scored 43 points against Colgate
University, running for six touchdowns and
kicking seven extra points. The Orangemen,
emerging as a national power, won seven games
and lost but one for the season and accepted an
invitation to play in the Cotton Bowl.

As his team prepared for the bowl game,
Brown once again felt the sting of racism. The
game would be played in Dallas, Texas, the
home of the Cotton Bowl. It was the first time

that Jim would play in the South, where segregation was still the law of the land. Throughout the southern states, blacks were forbidden to eat in many restaurants. They could not use restrooms or drink from water fountains designated for whites only. White hotels did not accept black guests, and there were very few black hotels. To avoid trouble, college teams often left black players at home when they played games in the South.

The Syracuse coaches booked a small hotel on the outskirts of Dallas and ordered the players to stay mostly in their rooms. In *Out of Bounds*, Brown described his emotions at the time:

> I understood their predicament, appreciated their extra effort. Typically . . . they would have found a nice black family for me to stay with. I would have practiced with my teammates, and when practice was done, they would go back to the hotel, I would return to the black folks. I would have been hurt and humiliated, because that's what racism does.

In the game itself, the Orangemen faced the powerful Horned Frogs of Texas Christian University. Although Syracuse had been voted the best team in the East, they were decided underdogs. Brown emerged as a one-man wrecking crew, rushing for 132 yards, scoring three touchdowns, and kicking three extra points. Syracuse put up a good fight but still lost, 28-27.

After finishing his senior football season, Brown turned to another sport that he had been playing at Syracuse—lacrosse. Big and powerful, and possessing great speed and tenacity, Brown was a terror on the lacrosse field. Smaller

Brown was perhaps the most fearsome lacrosse player ever.

opponents were helpless against the imposing midfielder. Brown would hold the ball close to his chest with his lacrosse stick and barrel down the field, scattering defenders who dared to obstruct his path to the goal. He earned All-American honors his senior year as the team went undefeated. Many who saw Brown play lacrosse considered him the best ever to have played the sport. His performance as a Syracuse midfielder earned him induction into the Lacrosse Hall of Fame.

Brown closed out his college experience by earning his degree. He was proud of his accomplishments at Syracuse. He earned All-American honors in two sports, graduated on time, and overcame racial barriers. His next challenge was clear—professional football beckoned.

4

THE BROWNS

After playing in a college all-star game in Chicago, Jim Brown headed directly to Hiram, Ohio, where the Cleveland Browns held their summer training camp. Jim was thrilled with the prospect of playing for the storied Browns and their legendary coach, Paul Brown.

The Cleveland football club originally played in the All-American Football Conference (AAFC), which began play in 1946. But after only four seasons, in which the Browns won the championship each year, the AAFC folded. Only three AAFC franchises—the San Francisco 49ers, the Baltimore Colts, and the Browns—were invited to join the well-established NFL. The Browns shocked everyone the first week of the 1950 NFL season by beating the Philadelphia Eagles, the league's defending champion. In their first year in the league, the Browns rolled through the regular season and edged the Los Angeles Rams

Otto Graham (carrying the ball) led the Browns to numerous great seasons before Jim Brown arrived in 1957.

30-28 in the 1950 NFL championship game. Led by strong-armed quarterback Otto Graham, the Browns captured the Eastern Conference title the next five seasons and claimed two more NFL crowns by winning the championship games in 1954 and 1955.

The Browns' domination ended when Graham retired after the 1955 season. The team stumbled to a 5-7 finish in their first campaign without the future Hall of Famer. Going into the 1957 draft, the team desperately needed a quarterback. The Browns had the fifth pick, but the two top quarterback prospects in the draft—Len Dawson and John Brodie—had already been selected when Cleveland's turn came up. Mouthing the old draft-day cliché that they were taking the best available player, the disappointed Browns picked Jim Brown. The Syracuse running back quickly signed a contract that paid him $15,000 his first year, which included a $3,000 bonus.

The NFL had only 14 teams at the time, which meant there were only a limited number of roster spots available for rookies. Older players were particularly protective of their friends on the team because once a player was cut, he rarely could find a job with another team. Veteran players went out of their way to make rookies look bad during drills and tried to rough them up during scrimmages.

Coming into the Brown's camp, Brown was competing with Ed Modzelewski, a well-liked player, for the starting fullback spot. The veterans put Brown to the test, but he took it in stride. Modzelewski soon sensed that he would lose his starting role to the rookie and began helping the young running back during drills.

The veteran fullback later remarked that he felt like a stand-in for Babe Ruth.

In the third quarter of the team's second exhibition game, Brown zipped through the Pittsburgh Steelers defense for a 40-yard touchdown run. When he returned to the sidelines, coach Paul Brown told the rookie that he would be the starting fullback. "I felt like I'd gone to football heaven," Brown recalled in *Out of Bounds*. Paul Brown had always been reluctant to use rookies, but Jim Brown started in his first NFL game—and in every game of his career.

The Browns never expected Jim Brown to be

Brown sits alone on the bench: It took time before the rookie was accepted by his teammates an immediate sensation. But in his first NFL season, Brown led the league in rushing yards (942) and rushing touchdowns (9). The rookie phenom turned a lot of heads in the ninth week of the season. Against the Los Angeles Rams, Brown reeled off 237 yards on 31 carries, breaking the NFL single-game rushing record. Riding the strength of Jim's legs, the Browns returned to their winning ways. They posted a 9-2-1 record and won the Eastern Conference. Cleveland's season ended on a sour note when they were mauled by the Detroit Lions in the NFL championship game 59-14. Brown ran for 69 yards, including a 29-yard touchdown run, in that game.

By most measures, Jim Brown had an exceptional rookie year. He won the Rookie of the Year Award and led the league in rushing. But by his own standards, he fell short. Brown's goal had been to play well *every* game. He played well some weeks but not every Sunday. Some observers around the NFL questioned whether the Cleveland rookie would last very long in the league. After Brown carried the ball 31 times against his team, Rams coach Sid Gillman warned, "If he carries the ball that much in many more games, he's got to wind up either punch-drunk or a basket case."

Gillman had a point. In the days before million-dollar salaries, artificial turf, and domed stadiums, the NFL was a much nastier place than it is today. Rough play was standard, the rules were much looser, and referees did not consider it part of their job to protect the careers of superstars. Every team gang-tackled ball carriers, jabbed them with elbows, threw forearms at their helmets, and tried to get their fists under the runners' face masks.

The Browns were a running team, and their best runner, Jim Brown, was a marked man. But he proved all the experts wrong; he did last. Brown never missed a game in his nine-year career. The rough style of the professional game suited his talents. A big, strong, muscular man, he was a dominant, unrelenting force on the field. Defensive players came to fear and respect Brown's forearm, which he used to fend off would-be tacklers. Brown also made sure that tacklers never got a direct shot at him. He would position his body so that he could absorb hits. If his progress had been stopped, he would lunge forward to gain a few extra yards and to avoid being speared by a flying tackler while standing straight up.

Brown also survived due to his intelligence. With each season, he learned more about the art of running. In college he often hesitated to survey the field and pick his route once he blew through a hole in the line. That tactic did not work in the NFL because defenders who had been blocked would pursue the play and tackle Brown from behind. After getting flattened a few times, Brown learned to keep moving upfield while deciding in which direction to run.

In a *Sports Illustrated* interview, Brown summed up his running strategy:

> In one-on-one situations, you break tacklers into categories. A lineman who's four yards away, you figure to put a good move on him and run around him. A linebacker is quicker and therefore harder to fake. If he's three yards or less away, you drop your shoulder and give it all you got. If he's a defensive back, you just run right over him.

Cleveland Browns coach Paul Brown (right) said, "Jim combined power, acceleration, speed, and great balance with an inner toughness that never conceded the slightest edge to anybody."

Brown, as with most players, had his game-day procedures. He would never drink water during the game, thinking that it slowed him down. He never responded to trash talking because he did not want to lose focus on the task at hand. He cultivated a quiet, determined demeanor, hoping to maintain an air of aloofness and mystery that would perplex the opposition.

Perhaps the strategy that Brown is best known for was getting up very slowly after being tackled and leisurely walking back to the huddle. Some people said that he was lazy; others claimed that he was grandstanding. But his slow movements were calculated. When NFL defenders saw a back get up slowly, they immediately thought that he was hurt. Maybe his head was ringing, maybe he was tired or out of breath. Maybe one more hard shot would put him out of the game. When they spotted a runner acting sluggishly, defenders would hit him twice as hard the next time he had the ball. By getting up slowly on every play, Brown confused the opposition. They never knew when he really was hurt because he got up the same way every time. Play after play, Brown would drag himself back to the huddle, looking as if he did not have an ounce of strength left. Then on the next snap, he would take the ball and charge through the defense for another big gain. "I give all my energy when it's required," he once remarked, "and when it isn't, I move easily."

For the next four seasons, Brown led the NFL in rushing. In 1958, he ran for 1,527 yards, shattering Steve Van Buren's NFL season rushing mark. He led the league in rushing touchdowns with 17, total touchdowns with 18, and scoring with 108 points. For this effort he won the Jim Thorpe Trophy, awarded each year to the league's outstanding player. But the Browns' season ended in disappointment when they lost to the New York Giants 10-0 in a playoff game for the Eastern Conference title. The only NFL team that consistently had success in stopping Jim Brown held the league's best runner to 86 yards for the game.

In 1959, Brown ran for 1,329 yards and led the league in rushing touchdowns and total touchdowns with 14. In a game against the Colts, he scored five touchdowns. But the Browns finished the season at 7-5, second behind the Giants in the East. In the final game of the season, the Browns suffered a 48-7 loss to the Giants, the worst defeat in the club's 14-year history. Jim Brown was kicked in the head in the first quarter. When the dazed runner could not remember his assignments, quarterback Milt Plum escorted him to the sidelines. It was the only time in Brown's career that he ever left the field during a game. He returned to play in the second half but had little effect on the game.

Brown led the NFL in rushing again in 1960, rolling up 1,257 yards. The Browns posted an 8-3-1 record, finishing second behind the Philadelphia Eagles, the eventual NFL champions. The team ended its season on a positive note, however, outscoring the hated Giants 48-34 at Yankee Stadium.

Two expansion teams, the Dallas Cowboys and the Minnesota Vikings, joined the NFL in 1961. With two more teams in the league, NFL teams began to play 14-game schedules, two more games than in previous seasons. Change also came to the Browns organization. New York advertising executive Art Modell and several partners bought the Browns from the previous ownership group, which included Coach Paul Brown. Modell began to take an increasingly active role in the day-to-day operations of the team, and friction soon arose between Modell and Paul Brown.

On the field, Jim Brown led the league in rushing for the fifth consecutive year. In a game against the Eagles, he slashed his way to 237 yards, tying his own NFL single-game rushing record. But the Browns once again came up

Brown with his twins Kim and Kevin in 1961.

short. The team trailed the Giants by one game heading into the November 26th home game against their archrivals. The Browns lost the showdown, 37-21, and finished with a 8-5-1 record, third behind the Giants and the Eagles.

Cleveland was a good team between 1957 and 1961, compiling a record of 41-18-3. But, except for Brown's rookie season, they never could surpass the New York Giants. The Giants won the Eastern Conference in 1958, 1959, and 1961. However, the Western Conference teams— the Baltimore Colts in 1958 and 1959 and the Green Bay Packers in 1961—defeated the Giants in the NFL Championship games. The Philadelphia Eagles were the only Eastern Conference team to win an NFL championship during these years, beating the Packers in 1960.

In 1958, Brown married Sue Jones. The couple had twins, Kim and Kevin, and then another son, Jim, Jr. During the off-season, Brown worked as a marketing representative for Pepsi-Cola and spoke at banquets across the nation. At speaking engagements, he impressed everyone with his thoughtful, articulate observations.

Brown also emerged as a spokesman for civil rights. In the 1960s, the NFL provided opportunities for black athletes, but not equal opportunities. There seemed to be an unwritten rule in the league that a team could have only a few black players. And blacks clearly were not given a chance to play at certain positions, such as quarterback, center, and safety. Brown tried to change the situation for his black teammates, organizing them to fight against the double standards that they faced. Some people in the league labeled Brown as a militant. But Brown viewed his actions as an effort to secure fair treatment.

5
SUNDAYS
WERE MINE

Jim Brown entered the 1962 football season looking forward to another superlative year. But things went very wrong for the superstar. He broke his wrist early in the season but continued to play with the injury. During the off-season, the Browns had traded halfback Bobby Mitchell to the Washington Redskins for the rights to Heisman trophy winner Ernie Davis of Syracuse. But Davis was diagnosed with leukemia and never played a down for the Browns. Without another quality runner in the backfield, defenses keyed on Brown, and he managed only 996 rushing yards. Jim Taylor of the Green Bay Packers ran for 1,474 yards, bringing Brown's string of five consecutive rushing titles to an end. But the Cleveland back had his best year as a receiver, catching 47 passes for 517 yards and 5 touchdowns.

Without their superstar in top form, the

Runs like this 71-yarder on the first play from scrimmage against the Cowboys led to numerous victories, rushing titles, and opponents' frustration.

Browns struggled to a 7-6-1 record and third place in the East behind the New York Giants and the Pittsburgh Steelers. Over the past several seasons, the Browns had been a strong team, but they had been unable to surpass their Conference rivals, the Giants. Led by defensive standouts Andy Robustelli and Sam Huff and offensive weapons Frank Gifford, Y. A. Tittle, Kyle Rote, and Pat Summerall, the Giants dominated the Eastern Conference in the late 1950s and early 1960s. The Giants coaches devised intricate and innovative systems that their players executed with precision.

Art Modell (left) promised to work hand in hand with Jim and Paul Brown (right)—but he fired the legendary coach early in 1963.

Following the dismal 1961 season, some Cleveland sportswriters began to speculate that perhaps Paul Brown had lost touch with the young men whom he coached. Brown had been the only coach that the Browns had ever had, joining the team when it began play in the All-American Football Conference in 1946. Brown was so revered in Ohio that Cleveland football fans voted to name the new pro team that he would be coaching after him. Brown's teams at Massillon (Ohio) High School, Ohio State University, and the Great Lakes Naval base (which played during World War II) had enjoyed tremendous success. In the pro ranks, Brown became an innovator who introduced the analysis of game films, the grading of the performance of each player, and the use of detailed playbooks.

The Browns players, disappointed with the 1961 campaign, began to whisper among themselves that the team's offense had become too conservative and predictable. Jim Brown was one of those players. The team's star player had a complex relationship with his coach. Although many outsiders thought that the two men never got along, they shared a mutual respect and admiration.

Paul Brown had a cool, strict demeanor and demanded that his players focus on every detail in the preparation and execution of his game plan. He detailed every aspect of the team's regimen, on and off the field, and insisted that his players follow the rules and be model citizens. Jim Brown accepted many of the coach's rules because he believed that they helped the team win. But Brown occasionally flouted some of the rules. For example, Coach Brown preferred that his players not drive flashy cars. In his rookie season, Jim bought a purple Cadillac convertible and always parked it in the players' lot. The coach undoubtedly saw the car but never mentioned it to his budding superstar.

For his part, Paul Brown had problems with some of Jim Brown's qualities. He thought that the fullback had a lackadaisical approach to practice, never giving 100 percent in preparation for next Sunday's game. The coach questioned Brown's efforts when blocking for teammates, and he felt that Brown remained too aloof from his teammates.

Race was perhaps the greatest issue that separated the two men. Paul Brown had always hired black players, even before the practice became common. But, as with many white coaches, he did not fully understand the difficulties that black athletes then faced. The Browns, as with all NFL teams, practiced segregation when they traveled on the road. Black players roomed only with other blacks. If there were an odd number of black players, the team would assign one to a room by himself, rather than pair him with a white player. When Jim organized the other black players on the team, Paul accused him of stirring up racial discord. Jim, on the other hand, saw his efforts as an attempt to gain equal treatment for the team's black players.

After the dismal 1962 season, Brown and several other veterans decided to approach their coach to discuss making some changes for the next season, including opening up the offense. Art Modell, the brash 37-year-old owner of the team, found out about the planned meeting and told the players that he would handle the situation himself. He dealt with the matter by firing the legendary coach in January 1963. Under Brown, the team had posted a record of 114-48-5, had won three NFL championships, and had experienced only one losing season.

Jim was not surprised that Modell had fired the man who was the embodiment of the Cleveland Browns. Modell and Paul Brown had never seen eye to eye since Modell bought the team from Brown and his partners in 1961. A struggle for power and control over the team was in the cards, and Modell held the winning hand.

Modell appointed Blanton Collier as the new head coach. Collier, who had been the team's running-back coach, quickly invigorated the Browns. He hired former Browns receiver Dub Jones as offensive coordinator, and the two men overhauled the offense. They worked closely with

In 1963, Brown (top) shared the Jim Thorpe Memorial Award with Giants quarterback Y.A. Tittle.

quarterback Frank Ryan to strengthen the passing attack and installed new running plays for the backs. Collier devised a play that became Jim Brown's favorite—an option play in which the blockers would take defenders wherever they wanted to go, and Brown would read the blocks and pick his own hole.

Under the new system, the Browns improved their record to 10-4 in 1963. But the team still ended up behind the 11-3 Giants. With Collier's wide-open offense, Jim Brown had his best year. After eight games, the 27-year-old back had already run for 1,000 yards. He ended up with an incredible 1,863 yards for the season, breaking his own NFL record for rushing yards in a season. Brown lead the league in rushing yards, rushing average (6.4), rushing touchdowns (12), and total touchdowns (15). Following his blockers, including John Wooten, Gene Hickerson, Dick Schafrath, and halfback Ernie Green, Brown had nine 100-yard games and also ran for 223 and 232 yards in other games. For his efforts, the Cleveland fullback shared the Jim Thorpe Trophy with Giants quarterback Y.A. Tittle.

In 1964, Brown once again led the league in rushing, rolling up 1,446 yards. The Browns finally overcame their nemesis, beating the Giants twice and claiming the Eastern Conference crown with a 10-3-1 record. They capped off their splendid season by surprising the football world with their 27-0 shutout over the heavily-favored Baltimore Colts in the NFL Championship game. Each player received $8,052 as his winner's share.

The following season, the Browns looked ready to repeat as champions. They rolled

through the 1965 regular season with an 11-3 mark. Jim Brown rang up his third straight rushing title, running for 1,544 yards and winning the Jim Thorpe Trophy as the NFL's most valuable player. He scored 17 rushing touchdowns and 21 total touchdowns. But in the NFL championship game, the Browns faltered on a frigid day in Green Bay. On icy, muddy Lambeau Field, Jim Brown managed to gain only 50 yards in 12 rushing attempts and 44 yards on 3 catches. Meanwhile, Packers runners Jim Taylor and Paul Hornung sustained drives by grinding out first down after first down. The Browns trailed only 13-12 at the half, but Coach Vince Lombardi's ball control offense and stingy de-

Brown in his last game. As one opponent put it, "He says he isn't Superman. What he really means is Superman isn't Jimmy Brown."

fense carried the Packers to a 23-12 victory.

The 1965 championship game marked the final appearance of Jim Brown on an NFL field. In spring 1966, he wrote to Art Modell, informing the Browns owner that he was retiring.

Jim had decided to pursue a new career—acting. He had previously appeared in the movie *Rio Conchos*, and he had landed a starring role in a new action film, *The Dirty Dozen*, which was filming in London.

Believing that Brown was merely using the movie as a ploy to ask for a higher salary, Modell threatened to fine Brown $100 for each day of training camp that he missed. Modell should have known better. Brown had never haggled over money, had never sought to renegotiate his contract, had never been a hold-out. This was not about money; Brown really wanted to retire. Dressed in army fatigues, his costume for *The Dirty Dozen*, Brown held a news conference in London to officially announce his retirement.

Back in Cleveland, fans slowly began to accept that the great Jim Brown was never going to run the ball for their beloved Browns again. While some fans worried how the team would fare without Brown, others assessed his brilliant career. When he retired, Brown held the record in virtually every category for a rusher. The records included:

- Most seasons leading the league in rushing, career (8)
- Most attempts, career (2,359)
- Most yards gained, career (12,312)
- Highest average rushing gain, career (5.22 yards per carry)
- Most touchdowns rushing, career (106)
- Most touchdowns, career (126)
- Most rushing yards, season (1,863)

Later NFL runners, such as O.J. Simpson, Walter Payton, and Eric Dickerson, broke many of these records—with the help of artificial turf and 16-game seasons. Jim Brown still holds two important records: most touchdowns scored in a career, and highest average rushing gain in a career. Of all the running backs in NFL history who have carried the ball more than 1,000 times—including Gale Sayers, Simpson, Franco Harris, Payton, Marcus Allen, and Dickerson— only Brown has averaged more than five yards a carry. But statistics and records do not fully capture the essence of Brown's career. As one admirer of Brown's talent, sportswriter Mike Lupica, wrote in a 1989 article in *Gentlemen's Quarterly*, "Tell me that anyone was better than Jim Brown at carrying a football and I will tell you that you are wrong."

In *Out of Bounds*, Brown looked back on his career and summed up his attitude as a runner:

> "Sundays were mine. . . . I thought, one break, maybe two, I'd run wild. By the time I walked on the field I thought I was God. Don't kid yourself: Walter Payton, Gale Sayers, O.J. Simpson—all top runners have felt the same way."

Fans still ponder what heights Jim Brown might have reached if he had played a few more Sundays.

6

MOVIES AND REAL LIFE

At age 30, Jim Brown embarked on a new career in film. He had previously appeared in a western, *Rio Conchos* (1964), in which he portrayed a Civil War officer turned cowboy. The movie's director, impressed with Brown's work, suggested that the football star hire a film agent. Brown did just that. His agent quickly landed him a three-movie deal with Paramount Pictures, which promised Brown more money than he made playing football. (At the peak of his career, Brown made $65,000 a year.)

Brown's second and most memorable film was *The Dirty Dozen* (1967). Brown portrayed one of the 12 criminals used by the Allies for a special mission behind enemy lines during World War II. The film boasted a superb cast, including Charles Bronson, Lee Marvin, Ernest Borgnine, George Kennedy, John Cassavetes, Telly Savalas, and Donald Sutherland. Brown's character—a strong, independent man—represented something of a breakthrough. At that

Jim Brown in a scene from the movie Ice Station Zebra.

time, Hollywood did not offer many serious roles to blacks.

In his film career, Brown played gangsters, bosses, cowboys, and lovers—none of which had been traditional roles for black actors. Studio executives wanted to capitalize on Brown's image as a macho football player, and they usually cast him in tough-guy roles. They also made him a leading man. In *The Split* (1968), Brown portrayed the boss of a robbery plot, giving orders to the film's white co-stars.

Virile, handsome, and muscular, Brown soon became Hollywood's first black male sex symbol. He played opposite several of Hollywood's most prominent actresses. In *100 Rifles* (1969), he had a torrid love scene with sex goddess Raquel Welch. Because it was the first American film in which a black man had a love scene with a white woman, the movie stirred up a minor controversy. Brown also had love scenes with Yvette Mimieux in *Dark of the Sun* (1968), Jacqueline Bisset in *The Grasshopper* (1970), and Stella Stevens in *Black Gunn* (1972).

In his first four years as an actor, Brown made eight films. He starred in thrillers, such as *Ice Station Zebra* (1968), and westerns, such as *El Condor* (1970). One of his movies, *Tick, Tick, Tick* (1970), a thoughtful film exploring racial issues, received rave reviews from such prestigious publications as *The New York Times*. He then made several action films aimed primarily at black audiences, such as *Slaughter* (1972), *Slaughter's Big Rip-off* (1973), and *Black Gunn* (1972).

The former football star enjoyed making movies. He made good money, worked with talented people, and did not get hit by lineback-

ers. But acting did not provide the same thrills as football. In *Out of Bounds*, Brown provided his view of the acting profession:

> Movies are pure illusion. The actual making of movies, because you're filming a series of contrivances, and contrivances take a long time to set up, can be painfully dull. Acting entails a lot of standing around, or sitting in trailers, punctu-

Making movies isn't all action and glamour, as Brown shows on the set of The Dirty Dozen.

ated by brief fits of work. It's mostly a passive process.

Brown's fast start in movie-making came to a screeching halt. By the mid-1970s, he no longer received calls from directors or producers. He had trouble landing roles in part because the mood in Hollywood had changed dramatically. In sharp contrast to the liberal, activist 1960s, the United States became much more conservative in the 1970s. Studio heads, seeking to reflect the temperament of the country, stopped financing movies with black leading actors. Hollywood suddenly had few dramatic roles for black actors. Only black comedians, such as Richard Pryor and Bill Cosby, seemed to get any major work.

Hollywood decision-makers were also reluctant to call Brown because of his involvement in several highly publicized scrapes with the law. Even during his football-playing days in Cleveland, Brown had found himself embroiled in legal difficulties. In 1963, an 18-year-old woman filed assault charges against Brown. When a jury acquitted the football star of the charges, the woman then filed a paternity suit against him. Although he won the suit, Brown later admitted that he had indeed fathered the child.

After moving to Hollywood, Brown kept getting in trouble. In one incident, a judge fined him for hitting a deputy with a forearm during a domestic dispute at Brown's home. In another altercation, a jury convicted Brown of assaulting a golf partner. He was implicated in several other assaults. But in each of these cases, the charges were eventually dropped. In *Out of Bounds*, Brown admitted, "I've slapped women and put my hands on men." But he contended that many of the incidents that made the headlines were untrue or greatly exaggerated.

Brown also gained notoriety as a ladies man (he had divorced his wife in 1970) and for the wild parties that he threw at his house. Rumors that sex and drugs were readily available at his parties circulated throughout Los Angeles. And many people in Hollywood considered his views on race as militant, especially when he became good friends with such controversial figures as Malcolm X, Huey Newton, and Muhammad Ali. Studio executives, aware of the sensationalist headlines and the public perception of the actor, steered clear of Brown and did not cast him in any of their films.

Although Brown could no longer find acting work, he kept busy, emerging as an ardent supporter of the black community. He became involved in several organizations that provided assistance to African Americans. Brown had earlier formed the Black Economic Union (BEU), an organization that emphasized economic development for African Americans. Under the motto "Produce, Achieve, and Prosper," the BEU opened offices across the nation in the mid-1960s. The organization aided young black businesspeople get their companies started by helping them acquire financing and technical knowledge. With the help of a $1 million grant from the Ford Foundation, the BEU assisted many businesses owned and operated by African Americans. One of these business, Ocean Productions, sought to produce movies by minority directors. Brown himself was president of the company.

Brown also served as Executive Director of Vital Issues, a program that taught prison inmates self-reliance skills. Vital Issues counselors showed prisoners how to set goals, make decisions, and control their emotions. They also provided the inmates with practical information on seeking jobs, handling family relations, and managing their personal finances. Many who participated in the program had never had the opportunity to develop life-management skills. Vital Issues gave them hope that they could turn around their lives. Vital Issues offered its program in prisons in Texas, California, and several other states.

Throughout his life Brown always spoke out against racism—to newspaper reporters, banquet audiences, TV talk show hosts, and anyone who would listen. In *Out of Bounds*, Brown revealed the impact of racism on his life:

> What I want every day is to live my life with spontaneity. To live a natural life. That sounds elementary, but as a black American, I don't have that. As a black American, I monitor almost everything I do. I must be careful of how I look, where I look, my body language. If I don't act the way a black man is Supposed To, I'll make the people around me embarrassed, injure their feelings, or generate their anger. I will create a Racial Situation.

Brown also spoke out against racism in the NFL, criticizing the Hall of Fame for ignoring deserving black players and pointing out the lack of black head coaches in the league.

Although he maintained only minimal contact with the NFL after retiring, Brown could not ignore football. In 1971, he was inducted into the Pro Football Hall of Fame in Canton, Ohio. Among the other seven inductees were Vince Lombardi, Andy Robustelli, Y.A. Tittle, and Norm

Van Brocklin. In 1982, he served as grand marshall of Super Bowl XVI, in which the San Francisco 49ers faced the Cincinnati Bengals.

The next year, Brown jokingly remarked on a radio show that he was thinking about returning to the NFL to prevent the Steelers' Franco Harris from surpassing his career rushing record. Reporters took his offhand remark seriously, and his purported comeback became headline news. Eighteen years after his retirement, Brown appeared on the cover of *Sports Illustrated* above a headline trumpeting, "Just What The Boring NFL Needed." Harris never did break Brown's record. But Chicago Bears running back Walter Payton surpassed Brown in 1984 and ended his 13-year career in 1987 with a total of 16,726 rushing yards.

Brown continued to focus his efforts on improving conditions in the black community. In the early 1990s, Brown started Amer-I-Can, a self-help program aimed at prison inmates and street gang members. In many ways similar to the Vital Issues program, Amer-I-Can seeks to teach young people life-management skills. The counselors, known as facilitators, advise those who enroll in the program on how to find a job, assume family responsibilities, and resolve conflicts. Brown himself walks the streets where gang wars rage to promote Amer-I-Can. Gang members respect the former football player. As he told a *Newsweek* reporter, "I'm not afraid of them. It's no different with gangbangers than it is with big linebackers."

When not working on Amer-I-Can projects, Brown continues to act. He appeared in two popular movies in the 1990s: *Running Man*, an action picture starring Arnold Schwarzenegger,

Jim Brown acknowledged, "God gave me something special.... I was special. I didn't always know it."

and *I'm Gonna Git You Sucka*, a spoof on black action films directed by Keenen Ivory Wayans. And he still makes money starring in low-budget action films made for overseas markets.

Many professional athletes have trouble coping with life after retirement. They often cannot duplicate the excellence that they enjoyed in their athletic career and can find comfort only in reliving their athletic feats. Although fiercely proud of his achievements on the gridiron, Jim Brown refuses to lose himself in the memories of his past glory. He looks only to the future, committed to the human development of himself and others.

JIM BROWN:
A CHRONOLOGY

1936	James Nathaniel Brown born on February 17 on St. Simons Island, Georgia
1944	Moves to Long Island, New York, to join his mother
1951–53	Emerges as star athlete in football, basketball, track, and lacrosse at Manhasset High School
1953	Arrives at Syracuse University as a freshman
1956–57	Earns All-American honors in football and lacrosse in his senior year at Syracuse
1957	Starts pro career with Cleveland Browns; leads NFL in rushing; breaks NFL single-game rushing record; wins Rookie of the Year Award
1958	Leads NFL in rushing; breaks NFL single-season rushing record with 1,527 yards; receives Jim Thorpe Trophy as outstanding NFL player; marries Sue Jones
1959	Leads NFL in rushing; scores five touchdowns in one game
1960	Leads NFL in rushing
1961	Leads NFL in rushing; ties own single-game rushing record
1962	Plays season with injured wrist; fails to lead NFL in rushing for only time in career
1963	Leads NFL in rushing; breaks his own NFL record with 1,863 yards; receives Jim Thorpe Trophy, along with Y.A. Tittle
1964	Leads NFL in rushing; helps Browns win NFL championship
1965	Leads in NFL in rushing; receives Jim Thorpe Trophy
1966	Scores three touchdowns in final Pro Bowl appearance; announces retirement from NFL on set of *The Dirty Dozen*, his second movie
1971	Inducted into Pro Football Hall of Fame
1982	Serves as grand marshall of Super Bowl XVI
1990	Founds Amer-I-Can
1992	Appointed to board of directors of Rebuild L.A.

STATISTICS

JAMES NATHANIEL "JIM" BROWN

YEAR	TEAM	G	RUSHING				PASS RECEIVING				SCORING	
			ATT	YDS	AVG	TD	CT	YDS	AVG	TD	TD	PT
1957	Cleveland	12	202	**942**	4.7	**9**	16	55	3.4	1	10	6
1958	Cleveland	12	**257**	**1527**	5.9	**17**	16	138	8.6	1	**18**	**10**
1959	Cleveland	12	**290**	**1329**	4.6	**14**	24	190	7.9	0	**14**	8
1960	Cleveland	12	215	**1257**	5.8	9	19	204	10.7	2	11	6
1961	Cleveland	14	**305**	**1408**	4.6	8	46	459	10.0	2	10	6
1962	Cleveland	14	230	996	4.3	13	47	517	11.0	5	18	10
1963	Cleveland	14	**291**	**1863**	**6.4**	**12**	24	268	11.2	3	**15**	9
1964	Cleveland	14	**280**	**1446**	**5.2**	7	36	340	9.4	2	9	5
1965	Cleveland	14	**289**	**1544**	5.3	**17**	34	328	9.6	4	21	12
Totals		118	2359	12312	**5.2**	106	262	2499	9.5	20	**126**	75

G   games
ATT   attempts
YDS   yards
AVG   average
TD   touchdowns
CT   passes caught
PTS   points

bold indicates league-leading figures

SUGGESTIONS FOR FURTHER READING

Brown, Jim and Steve Delsohn. *Out of Bounds.* New York: Zebra Books, 1990.

Brown, Paul and Jack Clary. *PB: The Paul Brown Story.* New York: Atheneum, 1979.

Cohen, Richard et al. *The Scrapbook of Pro Football.* New York: Bobbs-Merrill, 1976.

Gallagher, Robert C. *Ernie Davis: The Elmira Express.* Silver Springs, MD: The Bartleby Press, 1983.

Neft, David S., and Richard M. Cohen. *The Sport Encyclopedia of Pro Football.* New York: St. Martin's Press, 1990.

Olderman, Murray. *The Running Back.* Englewood Cliffs, NJ: Prentice-Hall, 1969.

Whittingham, Richard. *Saturday Afternoon: College Football and the Men Who Made the Day.* New York: Workman, 1985.

ABOUT THE AUTHOR

A lifelong Cleveland Brown fan, G. S. Prentzas is a freelance editor and writer who lives in New York City. He has written several books for young readers, including *Thurgood Marshall: Champion of Justice.*

INDEX

PICTURE CREDITS
UPI/Bettmann Newsphotos: 2, 8, 24, 32, 38, 40, 42, 47, 55; Courtesy Cleveland Browns: 10; Cleveland Press Collection, Cleveland State University: 13, 17, 35, 44; Courtesy Manhasset Senior High Library: 18, 22; Syracuse University, Sports Information Department: 30; AP/Wide World Photos: 49; John H. Reid III/Cleveland Browns: 59